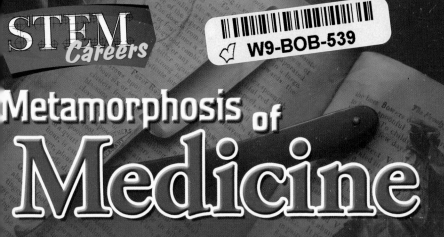

STEM
Careers

W9-BOB-539

Metamorphosis of
Medicine

Sharon Coan, M.S.Ed.

Consultants

Timothy Rasinski, Ph.D.
Kent State University

Lori Oczkus, M.A.
Literacy Consultant

Donald L. Coan, Ph.D.
Hydroponic Biopharming

Nicolle Kielman, RN, CEN

Publishing Credits

Rachelle Cracchiolo, M.S.Ed., *Publisher*
Conni Medina, M.A.Ed., *Managing Editor*
Dona Herweck Rice, *Series Developer*
Emily R. Smith, M.A.Ed., *Content Director*
Stephanie Bernard/Susan Daddis, *M.A.Ed., Editors*
Robin Erickson, *Senior Graphic Designer*

The TIME logo is a registered trademark of TIME Inc. Used under license.

Image Credits: Cover and p.1 Credit: Brooks/Brown/Science Source Enhancement By: Mary Martin; p.4 INTERFOTO/Alamy Stock Photo; p.8 Angelo Hornak/Alamy Stock Photo; p.10 World History Archive/Alamy Stock Photo; p.11 Mary Evans Picture Library/Alamy Stock Photo; p.12 Lebrecht Music and Arts Photo Library/Alamy Stock Photo; p.14 Wellcome Library, London; p.15 Al Fenn/The LIFE Picture Collection/Getty Images; pp.16, 18, back cover SSPL/Getty Images; p.21 Granger, NYC; p.22 PRISMA ARCHIVO/Alamy Stock Photo; p.33 Wellcome Trust Sanger Institute in Cambridge, UK; p.34 AP Photo/Paul Sakuma, Pool; p.35 Courtesy of Dr. Ahu Arslan Yildiz; p.36 age fotostock/Alamy Stock Photo; p.41 Michael Ventura/Alamy Stock Photo; p.42 World Economic Forum; all other images from iStock and/or Shutterstock.

Library of Congress Cataloging-in-Publication Data

Names: Coan, Sharon.
Title: STEM careers. Metamorphosis of medicine / Sharon Coan, M.S.Ed.
Other titles: Metamorphosis of medicine
Description: Huntington Beach, CA : Teacher Created Materials, Inc., [2017]| Audience: Grade 7 to 8. | Includes index.
Identifiers: LCCN 2016031450 (print) | LCCN 2016039650 (ebook) | ISBN 9781493836215 (pbk.) | ISBN 9781480757257 (eBook)
Subjects: LCSH: Medicine--History--Juvenile literature. | Medical innovations--History--Juvenile literature.
Classification: LCC R133.5 .C63 2017 (print)-| LCC R133.5 (ebook) | DDC 610--dc23
LC record available at https://lccn.loc.gov/2016031450

Teacher Created Materials
5301 Oceanus Drive
Huntington Beach, CA 92649-1030
http://www.tcmpub.com

ISBN 978-1-4938-3621-5
© 2017 Teacher Created Materials, Inc.

Table of Contents

Blood Out, Blood In

You feel exhausted, run-down, just plain sick. You need medical care. Do you go to a doctor or to a barber?

Silly question, you say? Well, that depends on the year. The history of medicine is a fascinating story of trial and error, innovation, and progress. Read on to learn how the field of medicine has evolved over time.

Flashback (AD 1170)

You see a blood-streaked towel hanging outside a barbershop, a sign that blood-letting is done there. The barber cuts your hair; then, with the razor he just used, he nicks a vein in your forearm and blood runs into a basin. He grabs the dirty towel from outside to apply pressure to stop the blood flow and bandages the incision with a rag. Soon, your wound becomes infected…and eventually you die.

Bloody Barber Poles

The red-and-white striped barber's pole is the modern reflection of the bloodstained towels that hung outside the barber/surgeon shops of the Middle Ages.

Fast Forward to Today

After a check-up, your doctor believes **anemia** is your diagnosis. To confirm, she writes an order for a blood test, and you go to a **phlebotomist**. He inserts a **sterilized** needle with a vial attached into a vein on the inside of your forearm. The vial catches your blood sample, and special equipment analyzes your blood. The results show you are severely anemic, so the doctor orders a blood **transfusion**. You receive red blood cells separated from a donation of your same blood type. Soon, you feel much better. Another test shows that your blood levels that measure anemia have improved.

The Origins of Medicine

People have always experienced illness and injury, and there have always been healers to treat them. Those healers shared their knowledge orally and in writing. In **Neolithic** times, a **shaman** chanted and danced around people who were sick. He brewed teas and made ointments and salves out of plants. These special potions were thought to help ease pain and cure common ailments.

Around 2630 BC, thousands of people worked to build the pyramids in ancient Egypt. Many workers suffered various injuries. Doctors splinted broken bones and prescribed medicines made from plants to those who had assorted complaints. Some physicians drove away pain by chanting spells.

As the Egyptian civilization was fading, the Greeks began to look for new methods of healing. Hippocrates talked with patients about their symptoms and then decided how to treat them. He had a wide variety of crude instruments and plant-based medications to choose from. He emphasized the importance of eating well and resting but did not focus on praying at the temple, as was normally emphasized for health.

The Romans, borrowing from the Greeks, built tremendous aqueducts and sewer systems. They did this because their doctors stressed the importance of clean water and healthy living conditions.

Egyptian Papyri

The reason we know so much about ancient Egyptian medicine is because of surviving documents. These were written on papyrus, a kind of paper. Because of the dry heat of the Egyptian desert, papyri buried in tombs survive today.

First, Do No Harm

Born in 460 BC, Hippocrates is known as the Father of Modern Medicine. Unlike other people of his time, he believed that illness had a physical reason and was not caused by evil spirits or the anger of the gods. Hippocrates believed that doctors should first try to "do no harm." This is part of the **Hippocratic Oath** that doctors still pledge.

HVMANI COR-
EX LATERE

ANA VESALII DE CORPORIS
PORIS OSSIV.
DELINEATIO.

HVMANI FABRICA LIBER I.
CORPORIS
POSTERIOR

HVMANI OSSA,
FACIE PROPOSITA.

Show Me a Body

Andreas Vesalius is known as the Founder of Modern Anatomy. His major work, *De humini corporis fabrica libri septem* (*The Seven Books on the Structure of the Body*), printed in 1543, has 700 pages, in 7 volumes, and contains many anatomical illustrations.

Leaving the Middle Ages Behind

Europe entered a time known as the Middle Ages after the Roman Empire **waned**. Barber/surgeons offered much of the health care of this period. Around AD 1450, things began to change. Two major events toward the end of the Middle Ages led to the growth and spread of medical knowledge.

The Printing Press

The first major development was the invention of the printing press in the 1450s. Inside a small print shop in Germany, Johannes Gutenberg used single, cast-metal letters to set a book for printing. He and other printers were the first to mass-produce books with this method. Because of his press, medical libraries thrived. Knowledge could be easily shared and gained.

Dissection

Andreas Vesalius began his study of medicine in 1533. During his career, he performed many dissections on human bodies. He even stole a **cadaver** from a body dump for executed criminals. Vesalius drew detailed pictures of what he saw as he worked on the bodies. Many of the things he observed did not match the writings from centuries earlier, which were based on dissected animals, not humans. Later, Vesalius published a book with sketches to show what he had learned.

THINK LINK

The invention of the printing press has been compared to the widespread use of the Internet today.

- ◎ How are the two alike and different?
- ◎ Which do you think has had a more significant impact on medicine?
- ◎ What are some positive and negative aspects of each?

wooden printing press

Disease Detectives

For centuries, scientists and doctors were unable to figure out why people became ill. Several discoveries, using science and engineering together, led to a modern understanding of germs. Without this understanding of the human body, we would not be able to treat or cure infections.

Around 1595, a father and son, Hans and Zacharias Janssen, bent over their worktable. But they weren't making the eyeglasses they usually sold. They had found a way to put two lenses into a tube so that objects could be magnified even more than with a single lens. Many scientists soon used this idea to observe and analyze small objects.

Years later, Robert Hooke spent hours drawing detailed pictures of what he observed through his microscope. In 1665, he published a book of his studies, *Micrographia*. One of the pictures shows the pores in cork. Hooke called these pores *cells*, not realizing he had coined the name for an important scientific concept.

flea engraving from Robert Hooke's *Micrographia*

Flea Glasses

Early magnifying glasses were used to observe tiny insects, such as fleas. So, these lenses became known as "flea glasses."

Curtain-Maker, Engineer, or Scientist?

As a teenager, Antonie van Leeuwenhoek was apprenticed to a cloth maker. As part of his work, he used a simple magnifying lens mounted on a stand to study cloth. He was hooked! Soon, he learned to grind lenses and build his own microscopes.

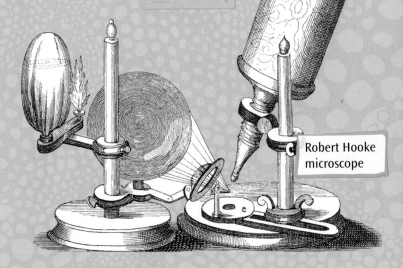

Robert Hooke microscope

Antonie van Leeuwenhoek's primary job was making drapes to hang in the windows of Dutch homes. But in his spare time, he did the work for which he is now called the Father of **Microbiology**. In his drapery shop, van Leeuwenhoek worked to make an even more powerful microscope than Hooke. Finally, he magnified an object 270 times. He was excited to be the first to see bacteria, yeast plants, and living things in drops of water. He even saw muscle fibers and separated cells flowing in blood.

Through all these discoveries, the stage was set for the intense study of germs.

Louis Pasteur

Easy as Picking Apples

"As soon as the right method was found, discoveries came as easily as ripe apples from a tree."

This quotation from Robert Koch shows how important the development of consistent methods or procedures is to scientific discovery. Using his own method of control-group experimentation, Koch found the bacteria that caused tuberculosis, a serious, deadly disease.

From Chemist to Biologist

In 1854, Louis Pasteur had just gotten a new job in Lille, France, and had hoped to continue his work as a chemist, studying crystals. But local farmers begged him to find out what was souring their wine. Using his microscope, he discovered that living organisms were the cause. He developed a process called pasteurization, which used heat to kill germs. He continued his studies of tiny living things and discovered several species of bacteria. He found out more about how germs are dangerous to humans, which led to the development of vaccines.

It's All About the Method

In Germany, Robert Koch set up a laboratory to work with Pasteur's ideas. He collected blood from local farm animals. His microscope showed that blood from animals that died of **anthrax** contained bacteria which were not in the blood of healthy animals. This gave him an idea for how to prove the bacteria were causing the disease. He injected one group of mice with infected blood and injected a control group with healthy blood. Sure enough, the first group died of anthrax while the second group lived. He experimented with several groups of mice before announcing his discovery in 1876. Other scientists used Koch's method, and by 1900, 21 organisms had been matched to the diseases they caused.

Will People Grow Cows' Heads?

Even before Pasteur and Koch did their work, the English doctor Edward Jenner developed a vaccine for **smallpox**. For thousands of years, smallpox had killed millions of people around the world. In 1796, Jenner noticed that cow maids who worked with animals that had cowpox did not contract bad cases of smallpox. He began giving people shots of pus from the poxes on sick cows. People who got the shot did not get smallpox. But Jenner was ridiculed for this discovery. A cartoon showed **inoculated** people sprouting cows' heads! He got the last laugh, though, because smallpox has been completely eliminated from the world today.

Polio

Jonas Salk developed the first **polio** vaccine in 1954. He pioneered the use of a "killed-virus" vaccine instead of using the live virus like most of his **contemporaries**. He first used it on himself and his family. Today, the World Health Organization is working to eradicate polio worldwide. Right now, they are 99% of the way there!

STOP! THINK...

- Can you find the doctor in the drawing? What is he doing?
- Why do you think people are still lined up when those who have been inoculated have such strange growths?
- Why did the artist create this cartoon? What is its message?

Medicine in the 1800s

In the 1800s, three major problems had to be overcome before complex internal surgeries could happen. First, cleanliness was a priority. Doctors began putting Pasteur's work with germs into practice. Before surgery, they washed their hands with disinfectant and put on surgical gloves. Because of these precautions, patients were less prone to infection.

Second, surgeons had to find a way to stop pain during surgery. A screaming patient was not easy to work on! Ether was used for the first time in 1842. This was a chemical that put the patient to sleep so that no pain would be felt during surgery.

Third, methods to stop bleeding during surgery were found. A small, heated tool cauterized, or burned closed, small blood vessels. The surgeon clamped and sutured large vessels. In the past, doctors had poured hot oil into wounds to stop the bleeding. Many times, patients died from the trauma of the experience.

Dr. William Thomas Green Morton performs the first successful dental surgery using ether.

All these improvements made for more comfortable patients and more successful doctors.

Florence Nightingale

Florence Nightingale was a nurse and later a famous health-care reformer. She was sent to a military hospital in 1854. Conditions there were horrendous. There were filthy patients, rodents and bugs everywhere, polluted water, and no consistent care. She and her team of nurses worked to fix the situation. They scrubbed the hospital, provided care around the clock, set up a kitchen and a laundry, and even established a classroom and a library. Later, Nightingale wrote a book that established the foundation for modern hospital care and nursing.

"Lady with the Lamp"

Nightingale was nicknamed the "lady with the lamp" by soldiers during the Crimean War (1853–1856). She was a welcomed sight at night when she would often check on patients with a lamp held near her face.

Medicine for the Industrial Age

Doctors needed to know more about what was going on inside living bodies to treat various illnesses. Dissection was not enough. The 1800s saw a surge in new instruments to help doctors improve the quality of care for their patients.

mercury thermometer and case invented by Dr. Allbutt

Thermometer

Dr. Thomas Allbutt was frustrated. He had no convenient way to determine just how high his patients' fevers were. The awkward tools of his time were a foot or more long and took 20 minutes to register patients' temperatures. Most sick patients could not wait that long. So, he decided to solve the problem. In 1866, he developed a six-inch clinical thermometer that registered body temperature in five minutes. Doctors everywhere began using this new and improved tool.

one of Dr. Laennec's original stethoscopes, made of wood and brass

Stethoscope

Normally, Dr. Rene Laennec would place his ear directly on a patient's chest to hear the heartbeat. But when he was examining a young woman, he used a large sheet of paper rolled into a tube. He placed one end of the tube on the patient's chest and the other to his ear. This way, he could clearly hear the heartbeat while avoiding any potential embarrassment to him or the female patient. And so, the stethoscope was born. Many versions followed, including a wooden tube and, finally, the two-earpiece version we know today.

How High Can You Go?

A sphygmomanometer is a tool used to measure blood pressure. In the first versions, a cut was made into a blood vessel. Then, an upright tube was inserted into the cut. Doctors watched the blood rise and fall as the heart pumped. The harder the heart pumped, the higher the blood would rise in the tube.

X-Rays

Everybody, it seemed, was experimenting with electricity. That's what Wilhelm Roentgen thought in 1895 as he studied the electrical current in **cathode ray tubes**. When the currents were directed through the glass tubes, he noticed a fluorescence on a screen across the lab. That was not part of his current experiment. What was going on? This led him to discover new rays. He named them *x-rays*, the *x* standing for unknown. He x-rayed his wife's hand and saw an image on a screen of her bones and wedding ring, but not her flesh. It didn't take long for doctors to recognize the usefulness of these images. Within months of Roentgen announcing his find, doctors were using the x-rays to see broken bones, kidney stones, and many other solids within the body.

Little Curies

Marie Curie knew about Roentgen's work with x-rays. When World War I broke out, she put her time and resources into developing and personally distributing portable x-ray machines to medical personnel on the battlefields. These machines became known as "Little Curies." Curie commented, "The use of the x-rays during the war saved the lives of many wounded men; it also saved many from long suffering and lasting infirmity." Curie died of leukemia, a type of cancer, likely caused by repeated exposure to the radioactive elements she used in her work.

Fate for Feet

In the 1940s and 1950s, some shoe stores installed fluoroscopes, which used radiation to check shoe-size fit. Salespeople and customers who used the machines were at risk for burns, skin conditions, and skin cancer. The machines were banned from most states by 1970 because of the radiation.

Danger!

Sometimes, there are risks when working with new materials and inventions. Years after the x-ray machine was first used, it was discovered that unprotected exposure to x-rays can cause burns and cancer. Today, patients are protected from the harmful effects of x-rays.

Marie Curie

THINK LINK

◎ What safeguards are in place to help prevent radiation-related illnesses from happening today?

◎ What other safeguards might be instituted?

◎ Should the potential of danger or harm keep people from experimenting?

What's in a Name?

Aspirin was the brand name created by the Bayer Company for their new drug. Here's how it got its name.

<u>A</u> <u>spir</u> <u>in</u>

A	spir	in
from *acetyl*, the agent added to make the drug less harmful to the stomach	from *Spiraea ulmaria*, the scientific name of the meadowsweet plant from which the **salicin** is derived	from the end of *salicin*, the active medical ingredient

The Chemistry of Medicine

Until 1900, most medicines were natural. They were made from herbs or other natural sources. Advances in research methods and the growth of factories during the 1800s changed that. Two medicines that evolved in this way are aspirin and antibiotics.

Aspirin

In 1897, a team of chemists was hard at work in the Bayer Company lab. For years, doctors had been using the meadowsweet plant as a natural painkiller. The team discovered that it was salicin from the plant that worked on pain. They figured out how to make it so that the salicin would not harm patients' stomachs, a problem when using the natural form. Bayer Company got the **patent** in 1899. In 1915, aspirin became available with no prescription.

Penicillin

Alexander Fleming, a Scottish chemist, arrived at his lab one morning in 1928. To study how **staphylococcus** caused infections, Fleming was growing bacteria in petri dishes. Looking closely, he saw that a mold had grown in the dishes. Amazingly, the mold seemed to have killed the bacteria. He found that the mold produced a substance that dissolved the bacteria. Fleming named the substance *penicillin* after the specific variety of mold. It became the first antibiotic. Soon, many antibiotics were produced in factories.

Health Care in the Age of Technology

The printing press put books into the hands of the masses, and hands-on dissections revealed the intricacies of the human body. Microscopes, labs, and imaging devices have helped find causes and cures for disease. These advances have evolved medicine. Today, technology is playing an ever-changing role in advancing the quality and efficiency of health care.

Electronic Records

When a doctor walks into an examining room these days, she does not carry the usual thick folder that has all the patient's records. Instead, she uses a computer or tablet to call up his electronic record. She records the results of her examination. Then, she orders a prescription and lab tests for him, all digitally. Later at home, the patient uses his computer to see the test results posted on his personal medical portal. No printed material is needed.

Virtual Dissection

Students in an anatomy class gather around a table. The table is a huge touch-screen computer. The professor clicks a button and a full-size 3-D image of a human body appears on the screen. He explains that they can look at all the parts, organs, and systems without cutting into a real body. The students can use this device to supplement their work with cadavers in the dissection lab. The work is much less messy and can be done almost anywhere!

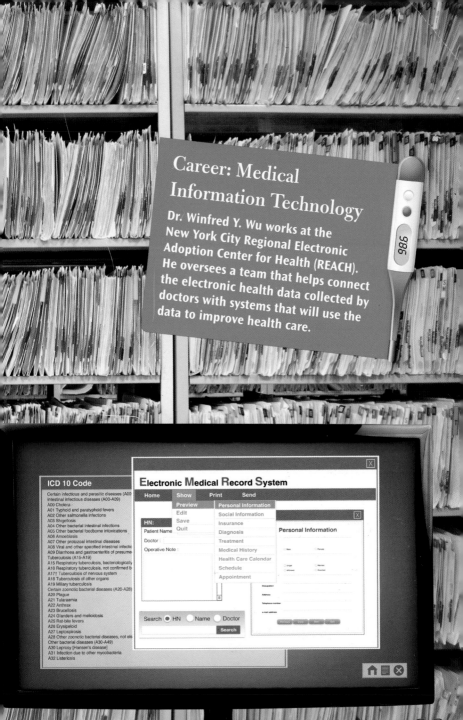

Career: Medical Information Technology

Dr. Winfred Y. Wu works at the New York City Regional Electronic Adoption Center for Health (REACH). He oversees a team that helps connect the electronic health data collected by doctors with systems that will use the data to improve health care.

986

ICD 10 Code

Certain infectious and parasitic diseases (A00
Intestinal infectious diseases (A00-A09)
A00 Cholera
A01 Typhoid and paratyphoid fevers
A02 Other salmonella infections
A03 Shigellosis
A04 Other bacterial intestinal infections
A05 Other bacterial foodborne intoxications
A06 Amoebiasis
A07 Other protozoal intestinal diseases
A08 Viral and other specified intestinal infectio
A09 Diarrhoea and gastroenteritis of presume
Tuberculosis (A15-A19)
A15 Respiratory tuberculosis, bacteriologically
A16 Respiratory tuberculosis, not confirmed b
A17? Tuberculosis of nervous system
A18 Tuberculosis of other organs
A19 Miliary tuberculosis
Certain zoonotic bacterial diseases (A20-A28)
A20 Plague
A21 Tularaemia
A22 Anthrax
A23 Brucellosis
A24 Glanders and melioidosis
A25 Rat-bite fevers
A26 Erysipeloid
A27 Leptospirosis
A28 Other zoonotic bacterial diseases, not els
Other bacterial diseases (A30-A49)
A30 Leprosy [Hansen's disease]
A31 Infection due to other mycobacteria
A32 Listeriosis

Electronic Medical Record System

Home | Show | Print | Send

Show menu:
Preview
Edit
Save
Quit

Personal Information
Social Information
Insurance
Diagnosis
Treatment
Medical History
Health Care Calendar
Schedule
Appointment

HN:
Patient Name
Doctor :
Operative Note :

Personal Information

Search ● HN ○ Name ○ Doctor
Search

25

Electron Microscopes

Right now, a scientist sits at a computer to view the images produced by the electron microscope next to her. A camera, much more sensitive than the human eye, sends digital photos from the scope to her screen. This type of microscope allows her to see tiny things she could not see by peering through an eyepiece. She is helping to find a cure for cancer by studying what causes it to grow.

Lab Tasks

Would you like to work in a medical laboratory? Here are some of the things you could do:

- Use sophisticated equipment and instruments, including microscopes and cell counters.
- Examine and analyze blood, body fluids, tissues, and cells.
- Identify bacteria, parasites, and other microorganisms.
- Cross match blood for transfusions.
- Monitor patient outcomes.
- Look for abnormal cells to aid in the diagnosis of anemia, leukemia, and other diseases.
- Assure the quality and accuracy of lab reports.

Modern Medical Labs

A few days ago, a throat swab arrived at a lab. It is from a patient who has been treated but is not recovering. Bacteria from the swab have been added to several petri dishes and allowed to grow. Then, disks with different antibiotics were added to each dish. Today, a technician uses a high-powered microscope to see what is happening. Sure enough, the germs in the dishes with traditional antibiotics continue to thrive as the bacteria have developed resistance to these drugs. But in two dishes, new antibiotics are killing them. The lab recommends one of these new prescription drugs to treat this patient.

Modern Medical Imaging

A patient has been experiencing pain in the abdomen. The cause is unclear to the doctor, so he orders a digital x-ray. Compared to the original x-rays, digital x-rays produce clearer images and emit less radiation. The x-ray shows something in the area of the gallbladder, but it's still not clear exactly what it is. So, an **ultrasound** is done. Ultrasonic pressure waves echo off the gallbladder. A computer turns the waves into images on a screen. The doctor can now see that the patient has gallstones, but it's hard to tell if they are blocking the bile ducts. To discover this, the doctor orders a **HIDA scan**. This scan will show the liver and gallbladder working in real-time, as opposed to the still images provided by other scans. The doctor is able to see the bile moving from the liver to the gallbladder and into the small intestine, so there is no blockage. With the aid of all this advanced inner-body imaging, the doctor and patient decide on an appropriate treatment.

ultrasound diagnostic machine

Career: Radiologist

Karen Reuss, M.D., is a women's imaging specialist at Newport Diagnostic Center, where she uses imaging to determine whether her patients have cancer or other diseases. In an interview, Dr. Reuss spoke of her work.

Question: What changes have you seen in radiology over the years?

Dr. Reuss: The most change has happened with the radiological equipment we use. Technology research and a strong, competitive market have produced increasingly efficient and accurate imaging machines.

Question: How has this equipment changed your work?

Dr. Reuss: I am excited about the new 3-D Tomosynthesis equipment we have. These machines rotate around the area being examined and take a series of images, which are then synthesized into a 3-D image. They are more efficient and comfortable for the patient than traditional imaging machines. Extremely clear images produced in three dimensions allow the radiologist to make very accurate diagnoses.

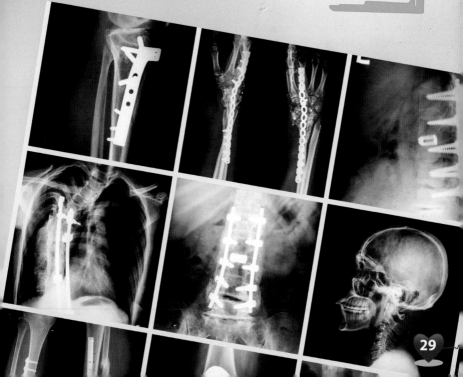

Ebola: Stopping an Epidemic

In 1976, a new virus is ravaging people in Zaire, Africa. Over the next 20 years, it infects people in several African countries. Doctors from around the world work to stop the spread of this deadly virus.

Outbreak in Democratic Republic of Congo
315 reported cases; 250 deaths

1980   **1990**

1975   **1985**   **1995**

A thermos containing two vials of blood arrives at a lab in Belgium. A note says the blood is from a nun working in Africa. She is one of 318 people who have contracted a mysterious disease and is at risk of dying. Dr. Peter Piot looks at the blood under a microscope and finds a worm-like structure that is huge compared to other microbes. This newfound virus is later named Ebola. Doctor Piot discovers that contact with infected people's body fluids causes the disease to spread.

An outbreak of Ebola occurs in western Africa and kills over 11,000 people. World health organizations send teams to help fight the disease. During treatment, they wear protective clothing, keep sterile work areas, isolate patients, and quarantine those who have been in contact with sick people. By early 2016, the outbreak is stopped.

2000

2010

2020

2005

2015

Outbreak of a new strain of Ebola found in western Uganda

Outbreak in Democratic Republic of Congo
264 reported cases; 187 deaths

First outbreak reports in the Republic of Congo
57 reported cases; 43 deaths

Outbreak in Uganda
425 reported cases; 224 deaths

Prescribing New Health Care

Since the early days of aspirin and antibiotics, more companies have become involved in the manufacturing of prescription drugs. Scientists in the field are always looking for new ways to produce and use them effectively.

When a **biopharmer** goes to work, he does not walk into a field. He enters a room connected to a sealed greenhouse. Before entering the main growing area, he puts on a biohazard suit to avoid contaminating his plants. His **hydroponic** farm uses a special method to collect the proteins produced by the roots of selected or modified plants. These are analyzed for potential uses. The biopharmer checks his tobacco plants, which are currently developing proteins that could be used in a medicine to fight the Ebola virus.

Growing Medicine

Some plants make substances that kill their enemies, such as bacteria. Biopharmers change certain plants so they secrete a desired drug ingredient from their roots. Then, the substance is separated from the hydroponic solution in which the plant is grown. It can be used to make a medication.

Personalized Medications

A woman has suffered a blood clot in her leg. Her doctor knows that she needs a blood-thinning medication. Current research has shown that a person's genetic makeup can influence the specific dosage necessary for blood-thinners to work correctly. So, the doctor uses his computer to access his patient's **genome** chart. It is part of her permanent medical record. Her **genes** show that she will need a higher dosage than most people. The doctor uses this information to guide his treatment of this patient.

Career: Bacterial Geneticist

Dr. Christine Boinett works in the Pathogen genomics team of the Wellcome Trust Sanger Institute in Cambridge, United Kingdom. She uses DNA sequencing and computer analysis to study how bacteria develop resistance to **antimicrobials**.

"Robo-Doc"

Seeing the doctor may soon involve a robot. There are robots that can help people eat and provide therapy for special-needs children. And an operation today may not always require a surgeon standing over a patient in an operating room!

Robotic Check-Ups

A young child in a rural area awakens with a rash and feels very hot. There are no doctors nearby, but there is a clinic staffed with nurses and technicians. Mother and child wait in the examining room until the robo-doc rolls in. A nurse connects the robot with a doctor at a big city medical facility. The robot accesses the child's medical records, collects her vital signs digitally, and sends them to the remote doctor. The doctor can see what is going on in the exam room and direct the visit via computer. A diagnosis is reached and medication is prescribed.

Microrobotic Pills

There is something wrong with a man's stomach, but the doctor cannot tell exactly what. She will have to do exploratory surgery or conduct extensive imaging tests. Soon, there may be an easier way. The patient will swallow a robot pill! A capsule, about the size of a vitamin, will contain a tiny magnet, a camera, a wireless transmission chip, and a set of mechanical "legs." It will travel where the doctor directs it and send images to the doctor's computer. Then, the doctor will know what must be done to solve the problem.

pill camera

ITH Technician

INTOUCH HEALTH

INTOUCH HEALTH

Career: Biomedical Engineer

Dr. Ahu Arslan Yildiz works at the Middle East Technical University, in Ankara, Turkey. She believes that science and technology should help people get better and make medical professionals' work easier. To that end, she uses engineering principles to develop innovative and affordable diagnostic tools that can be used in remote parts of the world.

Robotic Surgery

A patient lies on the operating table with an **anesthesiologist**, a surgical assistant, and a nurse nearby. But where is the surgeon? She is off to the side, sitting in front of a special computer. It has tools for manipulating the robot that performs the surgery. The surgeon directs the robot to perform very precise tasks in a small area of the patient's body. Only a small incision has to be made. The patient will have a short, relatively comfortable recovery, and the surgeon will not be tired from the long, physical labor that traditional surgery requires.

Remote Surgery

Robotic surgery can take place even when the surgeon is not in the room. In fact, he might be miles away. Neither he nor the patient had to travel for this surgery because the robot can be controlled from a great distance.

Nanobots

A researcher operates a set of magnets that surround the head of a rabbit. The magnets are moving a **nanobot** inside the rabbit's eye. The nanobot is the width of four human hairs. At the researcher's command, a needle extends and operates on the eye. The researcher hopes that very soon nanobots will be used in the most delicate human surgeries.

Career: Medical Robotic Engineer

Linda van den Bedem is a mechanical engineer by training. She wanted to build a machine that would help society. So she developed SOFIE, a robotic surgical system that solves some of the limitations of previous surgical robots. Her system is small, has an elbow joint in addition to the usual wrist joint, and provides force feedback, or counter pressure, so the surgeon can "feel" the surgery.

"Robo-Patient"

Even though great strides have been made in the medical field, there are still times when surgeons must amputate damaged limbs or remove sick organs. New technologies are helping amputees and organ-donor recipients to improve their quality of life.

Brain-Controlled Prosthetics

An amputee is excited because today he will receive his new **prosthetic**. His arm was amputated after a car accident, and he has spent weeks recovering. Electrodes are implanted in his brain, and a mechanical arm is attached to the amputation site. As he looks at the arm, the electrodes send signals from his brain to his arm. He sees it move. It will take a lot of work to become proficient, but once again, he has an arm he can feel and work with.

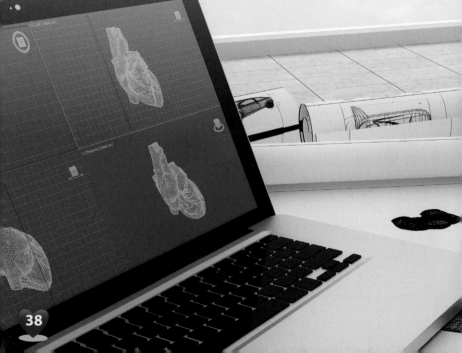

A friend paralyzed in the same accident is getting help from a special robotic suit, called an *exoskeleton*. It helps him stand and walk on his own. No more full-time wheelchair for him!

3-D Printing

Not far in the future, the previous scene is repeated, but this time the arm is flesh and blood, created through the process of 3-D printing. Down the hall, another patient is receiving a much-needed liver transplant. She didn't have to wait for a donor because her new organ was printed just for her. A third patient receives a hip replacement of real, 3-D printed bone, which matches her own bones exactly.

3-D printed heart

Career: Biological Engineer

Jennifer Lewis has her own lab at Harvard University. She works to "print" biology as a way to benefit society. She develops "inks" with living cells that can be used in 3-D printers to make human tissues.

The Human Genome

In 2003, a great feat of human discovery was completed. The Human Genome Project was an international effort to crack the genetic code for humans. The project mapped the entire human genome—the blueprint for our species. About 20,500 different genes were discovered. All of these are in the nucleus of every human cell.

cell

nucleus

chromosome

Enlargement of Chromosome

Enlargement of DNA Strand

The genes are located on 23 pairs of chromosomes. One of the first to be mapped was chromosome 22, which contains 500 to 600 genes. Many medical conditions are related to genes. Among them are anemia, some cancers, deafness, and heart problems. Researchers hope that gene therapy may someday prevent or cure these problems.

Career: Geneticist

Francis Collins directed the United States group that successfully completed the Human Genome Project. When it was announced, he stated, "It is humbling for me and awe-inspiring to realize that we have caught the first glimpse of our own instruction book." He and other geneticists continue to work to understand how information about our genes can be utilized for medical purposes.

These are the four chemical bases that make up a person's DNA.

• cytosine
• guanine
thymine •
adenine •

Your Career in Medical Technology

Does this sound like you…

You go to the doctor for your annual physical. You are more interested in the fact that he is using voice-recognition technology to record your results than in the results themselves.

You are virtually dissecting a frog in biology class. It's really interesting, but you keep wondering how the programmers created the software.

Your little brother falls and hits his head. The doctor orders a CT scan. You're very glad to learn that your brother will be okay, but you also want to know what a CT scan is and how the machine works.

Career: Medical Technology Educator

Dr. Shirley Ann Jackson is president of the Rensselaer Polytechnic Institute, the oldest technological research university in the United States. She was described by TIME magazine as "perhaps the ultimate role model for women in science." She has worked to inspire young people, particularly young women and minorities, to build careers in science and engineering.

Your father has to have a hernia repaired because he lifted something too heavy at work. The surgeon says he will do a robotic **laparoscopy** with two tiny incisions. You sure wish you could watch to see how it is done.

If you are fascinated by the technology involved in the medical field today, then there is a career waiting for you. Whether you study engineering, computer programming, physics, chemistry, or any of the other sciences, there is a way that it can be applied to medicine. Go for it!

Glossary

anemia—an abnormally low red blood cell count

anesthesiologist—the person who gives the substance that produces a general or local loss of sensation

anthrax—a disease caused by a bacteria that affects animals but can spread to humans

antimicrobials—substances that destroy the growth or spread of tiny organisms

biopharmer—a person growing plants for the purpose of producing medicines

cadaver—dead body, especially one to be dissected for medical study

cathode ray tubes—tubes from which the air has been removed so that electrical signals can pass through

contemporaries—people living at the same time as one another

genes—segments of DNA passed from parents to children

genome—a full set of chromosomes

HIDA scan (hepatobiliary iminodiacetic acid scan)—a scan used to look at problems with the liver, gallbladder, and bile ducts

Hippocratic Oath—a pledge recited by physicians after earning their degrees to promise ethical care for their patients

hydroponic—a way to grow plants in a nutrient solution without soil

inoculated—having been injected with a weaker form of disease to resist infection from that disease

laparoscopy—surgery performed through a very small incision(s)

microbiology—the branch of biology that studies microscopic organisms

nanobot—an extremely small robot designed to travel through tiny areas, like blood vessels

Neolithic—period of time from about 10,000 BC to 2000 BC; also called the Stone Age

patent—a trademark or brand that establishes proprietary rights

phlebotomist—a person trained in the taking of blood samples

polio—a disease that strikes the nerves and spine; can cause paralysis

prosthetic—a man-made device that replaces a missing human body part, such as a limb

salicin—a chemical, derived from meadowsweet plant, used to make aspirin

shaman—a person believed to possess magic; acts as a go-between for the natural and supernatural worlds

smallpox—a highly contagious, serious disease that causes pus-filled bumps on the skin

staphylococcus—a sphere-shaped bacteria causing infections in humans

sterilized—to destroy germs, usually by high heat

transfusion—the method of passing blood to a person who needs it

tuberculosis—an infectious disease caused by a certain bacteria, especially in the lungs

ultrasound—using ultrasonic waves to diagnose or treat disease and injury

waned—became smaller in size and power

Index

Check It Out!

Books

Haddix, Margaret Peterson. 1997. *Running Out of Time*. Simon & Schuster Books for Young Readers.

Morris, Alexandra. 2016. *Medical Research and Technology* (Cutting-Edge Science and Technology series). Essential Library.

Noyce, Pendred E. 2015. *Magnificent Minds: 16 Pioneering Women in Science and Medicine*. Tumblehome Learning.

Swanson, Diane. 2010. *Crow Medicine (Jane Ray's Wildlife Rescue)*. Whitecap Books Ltd.

Videos

SciTech Now, Episode 218. February 5, 2016. PBS. http://www.pbs.org/video/2365660397/.

Websites

American Medical Association. http://www.ama-assn.org/ama.

Centers for Disease Control and Prevention. http://www.cdc.gov.

Try It!

The Centers for Disease Control creates public service announcements (PSAs) when they feel they need to educate the greater public about an illness or health issue. Research a public health issue you believe is important locally, nationally, or internationally.

- Describe the issue, giving details about its history and impact.

- How serious is this threat to people's health? Why is it important to educate people?

- Create a script for a 60-second PSA about this issue. You may invite other students to help you present your information.

- Rehearse your lines.

- Record your PSA in the format of your choice, and share with your class.

About the Author

Sharon Coan, former teacher and editor-in-chief for Teacher Created Materials, has written, edited, or supervised countless books for young readers. She became interested in medical technology when she was diagnosed with early stage cancer in 2008. During the course of her diagnosis, treatment, and follow-up, she experienced digital x-rays, ultrasound-guided biopsy, MRI, and genetic testing of tumor cells. She was involved in a longitudinal study testing a new kind of radiation therapy that delivered the radiation directly to the site of the surgery. She watched as her doctors converted from paper to digital records, which allowed her team to instantly share information. Today, she is cancer-free and living in California with her husband and near her two daughters and granddaughter.